T0151943

THE GAME OF LIFE FOR WOMEN
AND HOW TO PLAY IT

THE GAME OF LIFE FOR WOMEN

{and How to Play It}

FLORENCE SCOVEL SHINN

DeVorss Publications
Camarillo California

The Game of Life for Women
Copyright © 2003 by DeVorss & Company

ISBN: 9780875167824
Library of Congress Control Number: 2004116134

FOURTH PRINTING, 2014

DeVorss & Company, Publisher
P.O. Box 1389
Camarillo CA 93011-1389
www.devorss.com

Printed in the United States of America

Contents

THE GAME OF LIFE FOR WOMEN AND HOW TO PLAY IT

All power is given to each woman to bring "her heaven" upon "her Earth" through right thinking. This is the goal of the Game of Life.

CHAPTER 1

The Game

Most people consider life a battle, but it is not a battle, it is a game.

It is a game, however, that cannot be played successfully without the knowledge of Spiritual Law, and the Old and the New Testaments give the rules of the game with wonderful clearness. Jesus Christ taught that it was a great game of *Giving and Receiving*.

"Whatsoever a woman soweth that shall she also reap." This means that whatever a woman sends out in word or deed will return to her; what she gives, she will receive.

If she gives hate, she will receive hate; if she gives love, she will receive love; if she gives criticism, she will receive criticism; if she lies, she will be lied to; if she cheats, she will be cheated. We are taught, also, that the imaging faculty plays a leading part in the Game of Life.

"Keep thy heart (or imagination) with all diligence, for out of it are the issues of life." (Prov. 4:23)

This means that what a woman images, sooner or later externalizes in her affairs. I know of someone who feared a certain disease. It was a very rare disease and difficult to get, but she pictured it continually and read about it until it manifested in her body. She died, the victim of distorted imagination.

So we see, to successfully play the Game of Life, we must train the imaging faculty. A person with an imaging faculty trained to image only good, brings into her life "every righteous desire of her heart" — health, wealth, love, friends, perfect self-expression, her highest ideals.

The imagination has been called the "scissors of the mind," and it is ever cutting, cutting, day by day, the pictures a woman sees there, and sooner or later she meets her own creations in her outer world. To train the imagination successfully, a woman must understand the workings of her mind. The Greeks said, "Know thyself."

There are three departments of the mind: the *subconscious, conscious,* and *superconscious.* The subconscious is simply power without direction. It is like steam or electricity, and it does what it is directed to do; it has no power of induction.

Whatever a woman feels deeply or images clearly is impressed upon the subconscious mind and carried out in minutest detail.

For example: A woman I know, when a child, always "made believe" she was a widow. She dressed up in black clothes and wore a long black veil, and people thought she was very clever and amusing. She grew up and married a man with whom she was deeply in love. In a short time, he died and she wore black and a sweeping veil for many years. The picture of herself as a widow was impressed upon her subconscious mind, and in due time worked itself out, regardless of the havoc created.

The conscious mind has been called the mortal or carnal mind. It is the human mind and sees life as it *appears to be.* It sees death, disaster, sickness, poverty, and limitation of every kind, and it impresses the subconscious.

The superconscious mind is the God Mind within each of us and is the realm of perfect ideas. In it, is the "perfect pattern" spoken of by Plato, or *the Divine Design*, for there is a Divine Design for each person. "There is a place that you are to fill and no one else can fill, something you are to do, which no one else can do."

There is a perfect picture of this in the superconscious mind. It usually flashes across the conscious as an unattainable ideal — "something too good to be true."

In reality it is a womans true destiny (or destination) flashed to her from the Infinite Intelligence, which is *within herself.*

Many people, however, are in ignorance of their true destinies and are striving for things and situations that do not belong to them and would only bring failure and dissatisfaction if attained.

For example: A woman came to me and asked me to speak the word that she would marry a certain person with whom she was very much in love (whom she called A.B.).

I replied that this would be a violation of Spiritual Law, but that I would speak the word for the right person, the Divine Selection, the person who belonged to her by Divine Right.

I added, "If A.B. is the right person, you can't lose, and if not, you will receive an equivalent." She saw A.B. frequently, but no headway was made in their friendship. One evening she called, and said, "Do you know, for the last week, A.B. hasn't seemed so wonderful to me." I replied, "Maybe A.B. is not the Divine Selection — another person may be the right one." Soon after that, she met someone who fell in love with her at once and who said she was *his* ideal. In fact, he said all the things that she had always wished A.B. would say to her.

She remarked, "It was quite uncanny" and soon returned his love and lost all interest in A.B. This shows the law of substitution. A right idea was substituted for a wrong one, therefore there was no loss or sacrifice involved.

Jesus Christ said, "Seek ye first the Kingdom of God and his righteousness; and all these things shall be added unto you," and He said the Kingdom *was within.* The Kingdom is the realm of *right ideas,* or the divine pattern. Jesus Christ taught that our words play a leading part in the Game of Life. "By your words ye are justified and by your words ye are condemned." Many people have brought disaster into their lives through idle words.

For example: A woman once asked me why her life was now one of poverty and limitation. Formerly she had a home and was surrounded by beautiful things, but she had often tired of the management of her home and had said repeatedly, "I'm sick and tired of things — I wish I lived in a trunk." She added, "Today I am living in that trunk." She had spoken herself into a trunk. The subconscious mind has no sense of humor, and people often joke themselves into unhappy experiences.

For example: A woman who had a great deal of money joked continually about "getting ready for the poorhouse." In a few years she was almost destitute, having impressed the subconscious mind with a picture of lack and limitation. Fortunately, the law works both ways, and a situation of lack may be changed to one of plenty.

For example: A woman came to me one hot summer's day for a treatment for prosperity. She was worn out, dejected, and discouraged. She said she possessed just eight dollars in the world. I said, "Good. We'll bless the eight dollars and multiply them as Jesus Christ multiplied the loaves and fishes," for he taught that *everyone* had the power to bless and to multiply, to heal and to prosper.

She asked, "What shall I do next?" I replied, "Follow intuition. Have you a hunch to do anything or to go anywhere?" Intuition means to be taught from within. It is a woman's unerring guide, and I will deal more fully with its laws in a following chapter.

The woman replied, "I don't know — I seem to have a hunch to go home; I've just enough money for airfare." Her home was in a distant city, and the reasoning mind (or intellect) would have said, "Stay in New York and get work and make some money." I replied, "Then go home — never violate a hunch." I spoke the following words for her: "Infinite Spirit, open the way for great abundance for _____. She is an irresistible magnet for all that belongs to her by divine right." I told her to repeat it continually also. She left for home immediately. In calling on a woman one day, she linked up with an old friend of her family. Through this friend, she received thousands of dollars in a most miraculous way. She has said to me often, "Tell people about the woman who came to you with eight dollars and a hunch."

There is always *plenty on a woman's pathway,* but it can only be *brought into manifestation* through desire, faith, or the spoken word. Jesus Christ brought out clearly that you must make the *first move.*

"Ask, and it shall be given you, seek, and ye shall find, knock, and it shall be opened unto you. (Mat. 7:7)

In the scriptures we read: "Concerning the works of my hands, command ye me." Infinite Intelligence, God, is ever ready to carry out our smallest or greatest demands.

Every desire, uttered or unexpressed, is a demand. We are often startled by having a wish suddenly fulfilled.

For example: One Easter, having seen many beautiful rose-trees in the florists' windows, I wished I would receive one, and for an instant saw it mentally being carried in the door. Easter came, and with it a beautiful rose-tree. I thanked my friend the following day and told her it was just what I had wanted.

She replied, "I didn't send you a rose-tree, I sent you lilies!" The florist had mixed the order and sent me a rose-tree simply because I had started the law in action, and *I had to have a rose-tree.*

Nothing but fear and doubt stands between a woman and her highest ideals and every desire of her heart. When a woman can "wish without worrying," every desire will be instantly fulfilled. I will explain more fully in a following chapter the scientific reason for this and how fear must be erased from the consciousness. It is your only enemy — fear of lack, fear of failure, fear of sickness, fear of loss and a feeling of *insecurity on some plane.* Jesus Christ said, "Why are ye fearful, oh ye of little faith?" (Mat. 8:26) So we can see we must substitute faith for fear, for fear is only inverted faith; it is faith in evil instead of good.

The object of the Game of Life is to see clearly one's good and to obliterate all mental pictures of evil. This must be done by impressing the subconscious mind with a realization of good. A very brilliant woman, who has attained great success, told me she had suddenly erased all fear from her consciousness by reading a sign that hung in a room. She saw, printed in large letters, this statement: "*Why worry? It will probably never happen.*" These words were stamped indelibly upon her subconscious mind, and she now has a firm conviction that only good can come into her life, therefore *only good can manifest.*

In the following chapter I will deal with the different methods of impressing the subconscious mind. It is everyone's faithful servant, but one must be careful to give it the right orders. A woman has ever a silent listener at her side – her subconscious mind.

Every thought, every word is impressed upon it and carried out in amazing detail. It is like a singer recording a song. Every note and tone of the singer's voice is registered. If she coughs or hesitates, it is registered also. So let us break all the old bad recordings in the subconscious mind, the recordings of our lives that we do not wish to keep, and make new and beautiful ones.

Speak these words aloud, with power and conviction: "I now erase and eliminate (by my spoken word) every untrue recording in my subconscious mind. They shall return to the dust-heap of their native nothingness, for they came from my own vain imaginings. I now make my perfect recordings through the Christ within — The recordings of *Health, Wealth, Love, and Perfect Self-Expression."* This is the square of life, *The Game completed.*

In the following chapters, I will show how you can *change your conditions by changing your words.* Any woman who does not know the power of the word is behind the times.

"Death and Life are in the power of the tongue."
PROV. 18:21

Ye, the Almighty shall be thy defense and thou shalt have plenty.

❖

CHAPTER 2

The Law of Prosperity

One of the greatest messages given to us through the scriptures is that God is everyone's supply and that a woman can release, through her spoken word, all that belongs to her by Divine Right. She must, however, have perfect faith in her spoken word.

Isaiah said, "My word shall not return unto me void, but shall accomplish that where it is sent." We know now that words and thoughts are a tremendous vibratory force, ever molding a woman's body and affairs.

A woman came to me in great distress and said she was to be sued on the fifteenth of the month for three thousand dollars. She knew no way of getting the money and was in despair. I told her God was her supply and *there is a supply for every demand.*

So I spoke the word! I gave thanks that the woman would receive three thousand dollars at the right time in the right way. I told her she must have perfect faith and *act* her perfect faith. The fifteenth came, but no money had materialized.
She called me on the phone and asked what she was to do. I replied, "It is Saturday, so they won't sue you today. Your part

is to act rich, thereby showing perfect faith that you will receive it by Monday." She asked me to lunch with her to keep up her courage. When I joined her at a restaurant, I said, "This is no time to economize. Order an expensive luncheon, and act as if you have already received the three thousand dollars."

"All things whatsoever ye ask in prayer, *believing,* ye shall receive . . . You must act as if you had *already received.*" The next morning she called me on the phone and asked me to stay with her during the day. I said, "No, you are divinely protected and God is never too late."

In the evening she phoned again, greatly excited, and said, "My dear, a miracle has happened! I was sitting in my room this morning when the doorbell rang. I said to the maid, 'Don't let anyone in.' The maid, however, looked out the window and said, 'It's your cousin with the long white beard.'

"So I said, 'Call him back. I would like to see him.' He was just turning the corner when he heard the maid's voice, and he came back. He talked for about an hour, and just as she was leaving she said, 'Oh, by the way, how are finances?'

"I told him I needed the money, and he said, 'Why, my dear, I will give you three thousand dollars the first of the month.'

"I didn't like to tell him I was going to be sued. What shall I do? I won't receive it till the first of the month, and I must have it tomorrow." I said, "I'll keep on treating."

I said, "Spirit is never too late. I give thanks she has received the money on the invisible plane and that it manifests on time." The next morning her cousin called her up and said, "Come to my office this morning and I will give you the money." That afternoon, she had three thousand dollars to her credit in the bank and wrote checks as rapidly as her excitement would permit. If one asks for success and prepares for failure, she will get the situation she has prepared for.

For example: A woman came to me asking me to speak the word that a certain debt would be wiped out. I found she spent her time planning what she would say to the woman when she did not pay her bill, thereby neutralizing my words. She should have seen herself paying the debt.

We have a wonderful illustration of this in the Bible, relating to the three kings who were in the desert without water for their men and horses. They consulted the prophet Elisha, who gave them this astonishing message:

"Thus saith the Lord — Ye shall not see wind, neither shall ye see rain, yet make this valley full of ditches."

A woman must prepare for the thing she has asked for *when there isn't the slightest sign of it in sight.*

For example: A woman found it necessary to look for an apartment during the year when there was a great shortage of apartments in New York. It was considered almost an impossibility, and her friends were sorry for her and said, "Isn't it too bad, you'll have to store your furniture and live in a hotel." She replied, "*You needn't feel sorry for me. I'm a strong woman, and I'll get an apartment.*"

She spoke the words: "*Infinite Spirit, open the way for the right apartment.*" She knew there was a supply for every demand.

She had contemplated buying new blankets when the "tempter," the adverse thought or reasoning mind, suggested, "Don't buy the blankets, perhaps, after all, you won't get an apartment and you will have no use for them." She promptly replied (to herself), "I'll dig my ditches by buying the blankets!" So she prepared for the apartment — acting as though she already had it.

She found one in a miraculous way, and it was given to her although there were over *two hundred other applicants.* The blankets showed active faith.

It is needless to say that the ditches dug by the three kings in the desert were filled to overflowing. (Read II Kings.)

Getting into the spiritual swing of things is no easy matter for the average person. The adverse thoughts of doubt and fear surge from the subconscious. They are the "army of the aliens" that must be put to flight. This explains why it is so often "darkest before the dawn."

A big demonstration is usually preceded by tormenting thoughts.

Having made a statement of high spiritual truth, one challenges the old beliefs in the subconscious, and "error is exposed" to be put out.

Make your affirmations of Truth repeatedly, and rejoice and give thanks that you have already received: "Before ye call I shall answer." This means that "every good and perfect gift" is already yours awaiting your recognition.

A woman can only receive what she sees herself receiving.

The children of Israel were told that they could have all the land they could see. This is true of every woman. She has only the land within her own mental vision. Every great work, every big accomplishment has been brought into manifestation through holding to the vision, and often, just before the big achievement, comes apparent failure and discouragement.

When they reached the "Promised Land," the children of Israel were afraid to go in, for they said it was filled with giants who made them feel like grasshoppers. "And there we saw the giants and we were in our own sight as grasshoppers." This is almost every woman's experience.

However, the one who knows Spiritual Law is undisturbed by appearance and rejoices while she is "yet in captivity." That is, she holds to her vision and gives thanks that the end is accomplished; she has received.

Jesus Christ gave a wonderful example of this. He said to his disciples, "Say not ye, there are yet four months and then cometh the harvest? Behold, I say unto you, lift up your eyes and look on the fields; for they are ripe already to harvest."

His clear vision pierced the "world of matter" and He saw clearly the fourth dimensional world, things as they really are, perfect and complete in Divine Mind. So a woman must ever hold the vision of her journey's end and demand the manifestation of that which she has already received. It may be her perfect, health, love, supply, self-expression, home, or friends.

They are all finished and perfect ideas registered in Divine Mind (a woman's own superconscious mind) and must come *through* her, not to her.

For example: A woman came to me asking for treatments for success. It was imperative that she raise, within a certain time, fifty-thousand dollars for her business. The time limit was almost up when she came to me in despair. No one wanted to invest in her enterprise, and the bank had flatly refused a loan. I replied, "I suppose you lost your temper while at the bank, therefore your power. You can control any situation if you first control yourself."

"Go back to the bank," I added, "and I will treat." My treatment was: "You are identified in love with the spirit of everyone connected with the bank. Let the divine idea come out of this situation."

She replied, "Woman, you are talking about an impossibility. Tomorrow is Saturday; the bank closes at twelve, and my train won't get me there until ten, and the time limit is up tomorrow. And anyway, they won't do it. It's too late."

I replied, "God doesn't need any time and it is never too late. With God, all things are possible." I added, "I don't know anything about business, but I know all about God." She replied, "It all sounds fine when I sit here listening to you, but when I go out it's terrible."

She lived in a distant city, and I did not hear from her for a week. Then came a letter. It read, "You were right. I raised the money, and will never again doubt the truth of all that you told me."

I saw her a few weeks later, and I asked, "What happened?

You evidently had plenty of time, after all." She replied, "My train was late, and I got there just fifteen minutes to twelve. I walked into the bank quietly and said, 'I have come for the loan,' and they gave it to me without a question."

It was the last fifteen minutes of the time allotted to her, and Infinite Spirit was not too late. In this instance, this woman could never have demonstrated alone. She needed someone to help her hold to the vision. This is what one woman can do for another.

Jesus Christ knew the truth of this when He said, "If two of you shall agree on Earth as touching anything that they shall ask, it shall be done for them of my Father which is in heaven." One gets too close to her own affairs and becomes doubtful and fearful.

The friend or "healer" sees clearly the success, health, or prosperity, and never wavers, because she is not close to the situation. It is much easier to demonstrate for someone else than for one's self, so a person should not hesitate to ask for help if she feels herself wavering.

A keen observer of life once said, "No woman can fail, if some one person sees her successful."

Such is the power of the vision, and many a great woman owed her success to a partner, sister, teacher, or a friend who believed in her and held without wavering to the perfect pattern!

By thy words thou shalt be justified,
and by thy words thou shalt be condemned.

CHAPTER 3

The Power of the Word

A person knowing the power of the word becomes very careful of her conversation. She has only to watch the reaction of her words to know that they do "not return void." Through her spoken word, a woman is continually making laws for herself.

I knew a woman who said, "I always miss a cab. It invariably pulls out just as I arrive." Her daughter said, "I always catch a cab. It's sure to come just as I get there." This occurred for years. Each had made a separate law for herself, one of failure, one of success. This is the psychology of superstitions.

The horseshoe or rabbit's foot contains no power, but a woman's spoken word and belief that it will bring good luck creates expectancy in the subconscious mind and attracts a lucky situation. I find, however, this will not "work" when a woman has advanced spiritually and knows a higher law. One cannot turn back and must put away "graven images."

For example: Two women in my class had had great success in business for several months, when suddenly everything "went to smash." We tried to analyze the situation, and I found, instead of making their affirmations and looking to God for success and prosperity, they had each bought a "lucky monkey." I said, "Oh, I see, you have been trusting in the lucky monkeys instead of God. Put away the lucky monkeys and call on the law of forgiveness," for a woman has power to forgive or neutralize her mistakes.

They decided to throw the lucky monkeys down a coal-hole, and all went well again. This does not mean, however, that one should throw away every "lucky" ornament or horse-shoe about the house, but she must recognize that the power back of it is the one and only power, God, and that the object simply gives her a feeling of expectancy.

I was with a friend one day who was in deep despair. While crossing the street, she picked up a horseshoe. Immediately, she was filled with joy and hope. She said God had sent her the horseshoe in order to keep up her courage.

It was indeed, at that moment, about the only thing that could have registered in her consciousness. Her hope became faith, and she ultimately made a wonderful demonstration. I wish to make the point clear that the women previously mentioned were depending on the monkeys, alone, while this woman recognized the power back of the horseshoe.

I know, in my own case, it took a long while to get out of a belief that a certain thing brought disappointment. If the thing happened, disappointment invariably followed. I found the only way I could make a change in the subconscious was by asserting, "There are not two powers, there is only one power, God, therefore, there are not disappointments, and this thing means a happy surprise." I noticed a change at once, and happy surprises commenced coming my way.

I have a friend who said nothing could induce her to walk under a ladder. I said, "If you are afraid, you are giving in to a belief in two powers, Good and Evil, instead of one. Since God is absolute, there can be no opposing power, unless a woman makes the false of evil for herself. To show you believe in only One Power, God, and that there is no power or reality in evil, walk under the next ladder you see."

Soon after, she went to her bank. She wished to open her box in the safe-deposit vault, and there stood a ladder in her pathway. It was impossible to reach the box without passing under the ladder. She quailed with fear and turned back. She could not face the lion on her pathway. However, when she reached the street, my words rang in her ears and she decided to return and walk under it. It was a big moment in her life, for ladders had held her in bondage for years. She retraced her steps to the vault, and the ladder was no longer there! This so often happens! If one is willing to do a thing she is afraid to do, she does not have to.

It is the law of nonresistance, which is so little understood.

Someone has said that courage contains genius and magic. Face a situation fearlessly, and there is no situation to face; it falls away of its own weight.

The explanation is that fear attracted the ladder on the woman's pathway and fearlessness removed it.

Thus the invisible forces are ever working for a woman who is always *"pulling the strings"* herself, though she does not know it. Owing to the vibratory power of words, whatever a woman voices, she begins to attract. People who continually speak of disease, invariably attract it.

After a woman knows the Truth, she cannot be too careful of her words. For example: I have a friend who often says on the phone, "Do come to see me and have an old-fashioned chat." This "old-fashioned chat" means an hour of about five hundred to a thousand destructive words, the principal topics being loss, lack, failure, and sickness.

I reply, "No, I thank you. I've had enough old-fashioned chats in my life; they are too expensive. But I will be glad to have a new-fashioned chat, and talk about what we want, not what we don't want." There is an old saying that a woman only dares use her words for three purposes, to "heal, bless, or prosper." What a woman says of others will be said of her, and what she wishes for another, she is wishing for herself.

"Curses, like chickens, come home to roost."

If a woman wishes someone "bad luck," she is sure to attract bad luck herself. If she wishes to aid someone to success, she is wishing and aiding herself to success.

The body may be renewed and transformed through the spoken word and clear vision, and disease be completely wiped out of the consciousness. The metaphysician knows that all disease has a mental correspondence, and in order to heal the body one must first "heal the soul."

The soul is the subconscious mind, and it must be "saved" from wrong thinking.

In the Twenty-Third Psalm, we read, "He restoreth my soul." This means that the subconscious mind or soul must be restored with the right ideas, and the "mystical marriage" is the marriage of the soul and the spirit, or the subconscious and superconscious mind. They must be one. When the subconscious is flooded with the perfect ideas of the superconscious, God and a woman are one: "I and the Father are one." That is, she is one with the realm of perfect ideas; she is a woman made in God's likeness and image (imagination) and is given power and dominion over all created things, her mind, body, and affairs.

It is safe to say that all sickness and unhappiness come from the violation of the law of love. A new commandment I give unto you: "Love one another," and in the Game of Life, love or good-will takes every trick.

For example: A woman I know had, for years, an appearance of a terrible skin disease. The doctors told her it was incurable, and she was in despair. She was on the stage, and she feared she would soon have to give up her profession, and she had no other means of support. She, however, procured a good engagement and, on the opening night, made a great hit. She received flattering notices from the critics, and was joyful and elated. The next day she received a notice of dismissal. A woman in the cast had been jealous of her success and had caused her to be sent away. She felt hatred and resentment taking complete possession of her, and she cried out, "Oh God, don't let me hate that woman." That night she worked for hours "in the silence."

She said, "I soon came into a very deep silence. I seemed to be at peace with myself, with the woman, and with the whole world. I continued this for two following nights, and on the third day I found I was healed completely of the skin disease!" In asking for love or goodwill, she had fulfilled the Law ("for love is the fulfilling of the Law"), and the disease (which came from subsconscious resentment) was wiped out.

Continual criticism produces rheumatism, since critical, inharmonious thoughts cause unnatural deposits in the blood, which settle in the joints.

False growths such as cancer, tumors, and cysts are caused by jealousy, hatred, unforgiveness, fear, etc. Every disease is caused by a mind not at ease. I said once, in my class, "There is no use asking anyone 'What's the matter with you?' We might just as well say, '*Who's* the matter with you?' Unforgiveness is the most prolific cause of disease. It will harden arteries or the liver and affect the eyesight. In its train are endless ills."

I called on a woman, one day who said she was ill from having eaten a poisoned oyster. I replied, "Oh, no, the oyster was harmless, you poisoned the oyster. What's the matter with you?" She answered, "Oh, about nineteen people." She had quarreled with nineteen people and had become so inharmonious that she attracted the wrong oyster.

Any inharmony on the external indicates there is mental inharmony. "As the within, so the without."

A woman's only enemies are within herself. "And a woman's foes shall be they of her own household." Personality is one of the last enemies to be overcome, as this planet is taking its initiation in love. It was Christ's message: "Peace on Earth, goodwill toward all." The enlightened woman, therefore, endeavors to perfect herself upon her neighbor. Her work is with herself, to send out goodwill and blessings to everyone, and the marvelous thing is, that if one blesses her supposed enemy, the other person has no power to harm her.

For example: A woman came to me asking to treat for success in business. She was selling machinery, and a rival appeared on the scene with what she proclaimed was a better machine. My friend feared defeat. I said, "First of all, we must wipe out all fear and know that God protects your interest, and that the Divine Idea must come out of the situation. That is, the right machine will be sold, by the right woman, to the right customer." And I added, "Don't hold one critical thought toward that woman. Bless her all day, and be willing not to sell your machine if it isn't the Divine Idea." So she went to the meeting, fearless and nonresistant, and blessing the other woman. She said the outcome was very remarkable. Her competitor's machine refused to work, and she sold hers without the slightest difficulty. "But I say unto you, love your enemies, bless them who curse you, do good to them who hate you, and pray for them who spitefully use you and persecute you."

Goodwill produces a great aura of protection about the one who sends it and "No weapon that is formed against her shall prosper." In other words, love and goodwill destroy the enemies with one's self, therefore, one has no enemies on the external!

There is peace on Earth for the woman who sends goodwill to all!

Resist not evil. Be not overcome of evil,
but overcome evil with good.

❖

CHAPTER 4

The Law of Nonresistance

Nothing on Earth can resist an absolutely nonresistant person. The Chinese say that water is the most powerful element because it is perfectly nonresistant. It can wear away a rock and sweep all before it.

Jesus Christ said, "Resist not evil," for He knew in reality there is no evil, therefore nothing to resist. Evil has come from "vain imagination," or a belief in two powers, good and evil.

There is an old legend that Adam and Eve ate of the "Maya, the Tree of Illusion," and saw two powers instead of one power, God.

Therefore, evil is a false law people have made for themselves, through psychoma or soul sleep. Soul sleep means that a society's soul has been hypnotized by the belief in sin, sickness, and death, etc.) that is carnal or mortal thought, and their affairs have out-pictured their illusions.

We have read in a preceding chapter that society's soul is their subconscious mind, and whatever is felt deeply, good or bad, is out-pictured by that faithful servant. A woman's body and affairs show forth what she has been picturing. The sick woman has pictured sickness, the poor woman, poverty; the rich woman, wealth.

People often ask, "Why does a little child attract illness, when it is too young even to know what it means?" I answer that children are sensitive and receptive to the thoughts of others about them, and often out-picture the fears of their parents.

I heard a metaphysician once say, "If you do not run your subconscious mind yourself, someone else will run it for you." Parents often, unconsciously, attract illness and disaster to their children by continually holding them in thoughts of fear and watching for symptoms.

For example: A friend asked a woman if her little girl had had the measles. She replied promptly, "not yet!" This implied that she was expecting the illness and, therefore, preparing the way for what she did not want for herself and child.

However, the woman who is centered and established in right thinking, the woman who sends out only goodwill to others and who is without fear, cannot be *touched or influenced by the negative thoughts of others*. In fact, she could then receive only good thoughts, as she herself sends forth only good thoughts. Resistance is Hell, for it places people in a "state of torment."

A metaphysician once gave me a wonderful recipe for taking every trick in the Game of Life; it is the acme of non-resistance. He gave it in this way: "At one time in my life, I baptized children, and of course, they had many names. Now I no longer baptize children, but I baptize events, and *I give every event the same name*. If I have a failure, I baptize it "Success," in the name of the Father, and of the Son, and of the Holy Ghost!"

In this, we see the great law of transmutation, founded on nonresistance. Through his spoken word, every failure was transmuted into success.

For example: A woman who required money, and who knew the Spiritual Law of opulence, was thrown continually in a business-way with someone who made her feel very poor. This person talked lack and limitation, and she commenced to catch those poverty thoughts, so she disliked this person and blamed this person for her failure. She knew in order to demonstrate her supply, she must first feel that she *had received* — *a feeling of opulence must precede its manifestation.*

It dawned on her one day that she was resisting the situation, and seeing two powers instead of one. So she blessed this person and bapized the situation "Success!" She affirmed: "As there is only one power, God, this person is here for my good and my prosperity" (just what they did not seem to be there for). Soon after that she met, *through this person*, a woman who gave her several thousand dollars for a service rendered. Her former associate moved to a distant city and faded harmoniously from her life.

Make the statement: "Every person is a golden link in the chain of my good, for all people are God in manifestation, *awaiting the opportunities given by others, to serve the Divine Plan of their lives.*"

"Bless your enemies, and you rob them of their ammunition." Their arrows will be transmuted into blessings. This law is true of nations as well as individuals. Bless a nation, send love and goodwill to every inhabitant, and it is robbed of its power to harm.

A woman can only get the right idea of nonresistance through spiritual understanding. My students have often said, "I don't want to be a doormat." I reply, "When you use nonresistance with wisdom, no one will ever be able to walk over you."

Another example: One day I was impatiently awaiting an important telephone call. I resisted every call that came in and made no outgoing calls myself, reasoning that it might interfere with the one I was awaiting.

Instead of saying, "Divine Ideas never conflict, the call will come at the right time," leaving it to Infinite Intelligence to arrange, I commenced to manage things myself — I made the battle mine, not God's, and remained tense and anxious. The phone did not ring for about an hour, and I glanced at it and found the receiver had been off that length of time and was disconnected. My anxiety, fear, and belief in interference had brought on a total eclipse of the telephone. Realizing what I had done, I commenced blessing the situation at once; I baptized it "success," and affirmed: "I cannot lose any call that belongs to me by Divine Right; I am under *grace, and not under law.*"

A neighbor contacted the phone company on my behalf and asked them to reconnect. My phone was connected at once and two minutes later, I received a very important call, and about an hour afterward, the one I had been awaiting.

One's ships come in over a calm sea.

So long as a woman resists a situation, she will have it with her. If she runs away from it, it will run after her.

For example: I repeated this to a woman one day and she replied, "How true that is! I was unhappy at home, I disliked my mother, who was critical and domineering; so I ran away and was married — but I married my mother, for my spouse was exactly like my mother, and I had the same situation to face again."

"Agree with thine adversary quickly."

This means, agree that the adverse situation is good, be undisturbed by it, and it falls away of its own weight. "None of these things move me" is a wonderful affirmation.

The inharmonious situation comes from some inharmony within a woman herself. When there is, in her, no emotional response to an inharmonious situation, it fades away forever from her pathway.

People have said to me, "Give treatments to change my spouse, or my friends." I reply, "No, I will give treatments to change you; when you change, your spouse and your friends will change."

One of my students was in the habit of lying. I told her it was a failure method and if she lied, she would be lied to. She replied, "I don't care, I can't possibly get along without lying."

One day she was speaking on the phone to a man with whom she was very much in love. She turned to me and said, "I don't trust him, I know he's lying to me." I replied, "Well, you lie yourself, so someone has to lie to you, and you will be sure it will be just the person you want the truth from." Some time after that, I saw her, and she said, "I'm cured of lying."

I questioned, "What cured you?" She replied: "I have been living with a roommate who lied worse than I did!"

One is often cured of her faults by seeing them in others. Life is a mirror, and we find only ourselves reflected in our associates.

Living in the past is a failure method and a violation of Spiritual Law.

Jesus Christ said, "Behold, now is the accepted time . . . Now is the day of Salvation."

Lot's wife looked back and was turned into a pillar of salt.

The robbers of time are the past and the future. If a woman's past keeps her in bondage, she should bless it and forget it. She should bless the future, knowing it has in store for her endless joys, and she should live *fully in the now*.

For example: A woman came to me, complaining that she had no money with which to buy Christmas gifts. She said, "Last year was so different; I had plenty of money and gave lovely presents, and this year I have scarcely a cent."

I replied, "You will never demonstrate money while you are pathetic and live in the past. Live fully in the *now* and *get ready to give Christmas presents*. Dig your ditches, and the money will come." She exclaimed, "I know what to do! I will buy some tinsel twine, Christmas seals and wrapping paper." I replied, "Do that, and *the presents will come and stick themselves to the Christmas seals*."

This too, was showing financial fearlessness and faith in God, since the reasoning mind said, "Keep every cent you have, since you are not sure you will get any more."

She bought the seals, paper, and twine, and a few days before Christmas, received a gift of several hundred dollars. Buying the seals and twine had impressed the subconscious with expectancy and opened the way for the manifestation of the money. She purchased all the presents in plenty of time.

A woman must live suspended in the moment.

"Look well, therefore, to this Day! Such is the salutation of the Dawn."

Be spiritually alert, ever awaiting your leads, taking advantage of every opportunity.

One day, I said continually (silently): "Infinite Spirit, don't let me miss a trick," and something very important was told to me that evening. It is most necessary to begin the day with right words.

Make an affirmation immediately upon waking.

For example: "Thy will be done this day! Today is a day of completion. I give thanks for this perfect day, miracle shall follow miracle, and wonders shall never cease." Make this a daily habit, and you will see wonders and miracles come into your life.

One morning I picked up a book and read, "Look with wonder at that which is before you!" It seemed to be my message for the day, so I repeated again and again: "Look with wonder at that which is before you."

At about noon, a large sum of money was given me, which I had been desiring for a certain purpose.

In a following chapter, I will give affirmations that I have found most effective. However, one should never use an affirmation unless it is absolutely satisfying and convincing to her own consciousness, and often an affirmation is changed to suit different people.

For example, the following has brought success to many: "I have wonderful work, in a wonderful way, I give wonderful service, for wonderful pay!"

I gave the first two lines to one of my students, and she added the last two.

It made a most powerful statement, since there should always be perfect payment for perfect service, and a rhyme sinks easily into the subconscious. She went about singing it aloud and soon did receive wonderful work in a wonderful way, and gave wonderful service for wonderful pay.

Another student, a businesswoman, took it, and changed the word "work" to "business." She repeated: "I have a wonderful business, in a wonderful way, and I give wonderful service for wonderful pay." That afternoon she made a forty-one thousand dollar deal, though there had been no activity in her affairs for months.

Every affirmation must be carefully worded to completely "cover the ground."

For example: I knew a woman who was in great need and made a demand for work. She received a great deal of work, but was never paid anything. She now knows to add, "wonderful service for wonderful pay."

"Her life should be full, and her cup should flow over!" This is God's idea for all people, and when people break down the barriers of lack in their own consciousness, the Golden Age will be theirs, and every righteous desire of their hearts fulfilled.

It is a woman's Divine Right to have plenty.
More than enough!

*Whatsoever a woman soweth, that
shall she also reap.*

CHAPTER 5

❖

The Law of Karma
and
The Law of Forgiveness

A woman receives only that which she gives. The Game of Life is a game of boomerangs. A woman's thoughts, deeds, and words return to her sooner or later, with astounding accuracy. This is the law of Karma, which is Sanskrit for *comeback*.

For example: A friend told me this story of herself, illustrating this law. She said, "I make all my Karma on my aunt. Whatever I say to her, someone says to me. I am often irritable at home, and one day I said to my aunt, who was talking to me during dinner, 'No more talk, I wish to eat in peace.'

"The following day, I was lunching with someone with whom I wished to make a great impression. I was talking animatedly, when they said, 'No more talk, I wish to eat in peace!'"

My friend is high in consciousness, so her Karma returns much more quickly than to one on the mental plane.

The more a woman knows, the more she is responsible for, and a person with a knowledge of Spiritual Law, which she does not practice, suffers greatly in consequence. "The fear of the Lord (Law) is the beginning of wisdom." If we read the word Lord as *Law*, it will make many passages in the Bible much clearer.

"Vengence is mine, I will repay, saith the Lord (Law)." It is the Law that takes vengeance, not God. God sees a woman perfect, "created in God's own image (imagination)," and given "power and dominion."

This is the perfect idea of a woman, registered in Divine Mind, awaiting a woman's recognition; for a woman can only be what she sees herself to be, and only attain what she sees herself attaining.

"Nothing ever happens without an onlooker," is an ancient saying.

A woman sees first her failure or success, her joy or sorrow, before it swings into visibility from the scenes set in her own imagination. We have observed this in the mother picturing disease for her child, or a woman seeing success for her spouse.

Jesus Christ said, "And ye shall know the truth and the truth shall make you free."

So, we see freedom (from all unhappy conditions) comes through knowledge — a knowledge of Spiritual Law.

Obedience precedes authority, and the Law obeys a woman when she obeys the Law. The law of electricity must be obeyed before it becomes a servant. When handled ignorantly, it becomes a deadly foe. *So with the laws of Mind!*

For example: A woman with a strong personal will wished she owned a house that belonged to an acquaintance, and she often made mental pictures of herself living in the house. In the course of time, the owner died and she moved into the house. Several years afterward, coming into the knowledge of Spiritual Law, she said to me, "Do you think I had anything to do with that a woman's death?" I replied, "Yes, your desire was so strong, everything made way for it, but you paid your karmic debt. Your spouse, whom you loved devotedly, died soon after, and the house was a white elephant on your hands for years."

The original owner, however, could not have been affected by her thoughts had she been positive in the truth, nor her spouse, but they were both under karmic law. The woman should have said (feeling the great desire for the house): "Infinite Intelligence, give me the right house, equally as charming as this, the house *that is mine by Divine Right.*"

The Divine Selection would have given perfect satisfaction and brought good to all. The Divine Pattern is the only safe pattern to work by.

Desire is a tremendous force and must be directed in the right channels, or chaos ensues.

In demonstrating, the most important step is the *first step, to "ask aright."*

A woman should always demand only that which is hers by *Divine Right.*

To go back to the illustration: Had the woman taken this attitude: "If this house, I desire, is mine, I cannot lose it; if it is not, give me its equivalent," the owner might have decided to move out, harmoniously (had it been the Divine Selection for her), or another house would have been substituted. Anything forced into manifestation through personal will is always "ill-got" and has "ever bad success."

A woman is admonished, "My will be done, not thine," and the curious thing is, a woman always gets just what she desires when she does relinquish personal will, thereby enabling Infinite Intelligence to work through her.

"Stand ye still and see the salvation of the Lord (Law)."

For example: A woman came to me in great distress. Her daughter had determined to take a very hazardous trip, and her mother was filled with fear. She said she had used every argument, had pointed out the dangers to be encountered, and forbidden her to go, but the daughter became more and more rebellious and determined. I said to the mother, "You are forcing your personal will upon your daughter, which you have no right to do, and your fear of the trip is only attracting it, for a woman attracts what she fears." I added, "Let go, and take your mental hands off; put it in God's hands, and use this statement: I put this situation in the hands of Infinite Love and Wisdom; if this trip is the Divine Plan, I bless it and not longer resist, but if it is not divinely planned, I give thanks that it is now dissolved and dissipated."

A day or two after that, her daughter said to her, "Mother, I have given up the trip," and the situation returned to its "native nothingness." It is learning to "stand still" that seems so difficult for a woman. I have dealt more fully with this law in the chapter on nonresistance.

I will give another example of sowing and reaping, which came in the most curious way.

A woman came to me saying she had received a counterfeit twenty-dollar bill, given to her at the bank. She was much disturbed, for, she said, "The people at the bank will never acknowledge their mistake."

I replied, "Let us analyze the situation and find out why you attracted it." She thought a few moments and exclaimed, "I know it, I sent a friend a lot of stage money, just for a joke." So the Law had sent her some stage money, for it doesn't know anything about jokes. I said, "Now we will call on the law of forgiveness and neutralize the situation."

Christianity is founded upon the law of forgiveness — Christ has redeemed us from the curse of the karmic law, and the Christ within each woman is her redeemer and salvation from all inharmonious conditions.

So I said: "Infinite Spirit, we call on the law of forgiveness and give thanks that she is under grace, and not under Law, and cannot lose this twenty dollars which is hers by Divine Right."

"Now," I said, "Go back to the bank and tell them, fearlessly, that it was given you, there by mistake." She obeyed and, to her surprise, they apologized and gave her another bill, treating her most courteously. Knowledge of the Law gives a woman power to "rub out her mistakes."

If any woman desires riches, she must be rich first in consciousness.

For example: A woman came to me asking treatment for prosperity. She did not take much interest in her household affairs, and her home was in great disorder.

I said to her, "If you wish to be rich, you much be orderly. People with great wealth are orderly – and order is heaven's first law." I added, "You will never become rich with a burnt match in the pin-cushion."

She had a good sense of humor and commenced immediately, putting her house in order. She rearranged furniture, straightened out bureau drawers, cleaned rugs, and soon made a big financial demonstration — a gift from a relative. The woman, herself, became made over, and keeps herself keyed-up financially by being ever watchful of the *external and expecting prosperity, knowing God is her supply.*

Many people are in ignorance of the fact that gifts and things are investments, and that hoarding and saving invariably lead to loss.

"There is that scattereth and yet increaseth; and there is that withholdeth more than is meet, but it tendeth to poverty."

For example: I knew a woman who wanted to buy an expensive overcoat. She went to various shops, but there was none she wanted. She said they were all too cheap-looking. At last, she was shown one the salesman said was valued at over a thousand dollars, but which the manager would sell her for five-hundred dollars, since it was late in the season.

Her financial possessions amounted to about seven hundred dollars. The reasoning mind would have said, "You can't afford to spend nearly all you have on a coat," but she was very intuitive and never reasoned.

She thought for a while and said, "If I get this coat, I'll make a ton of money!" So she agreed to the purchase.

About a month later, she received a ten-thousand-dollar commission. The coat made her feel so rich, it linked her with success and prosperity; without the coat, she would not have received the commission. It was an investment paying large dividends!

If a woman ignores these leadings to spend or to give, the same amount of money will go in an uninteresting or unhappy way.

For example: On Thanksgiving Day, a woman informed her family that they could not afford a Thanksgiving dinner. She had the money, but decided to save it. A few days later, someone entered her room and took from the bureau drawer the exact amount the dinner would have cost.

The Law always stands back of a woman who spends fearlessly, with wisdom.

For example: One of my students was shopping with her little nephew. The child clamored for a toy, which she told him she could not afford to buy.

She realized suddenly that she was seeking lack and not recognizing God as her supply! So she bought the toy, and on her way home, picked up, in the street, *the exact amount of money she had paid for it.*

A woman's supply is inexhaustible and unfailing when fully trusted, but faith or trust must precede the demonstration. "According to your faith, be it unto you. Faith is the substance of things hoped for, the evidence of things not seen," for faith holds the vision steady, and the adverse pictures are dissolved and dissipated, and "in due season we shall reap, if we faint not."

Jesus Christ brought the good news (the gospel) that there was a higher law than the law of Karma - and that that law transcends the law of Karma. It is the law of grace, or forgiveness. It is the law that *frees a woman from the law of cause and effect — the law of consequence. "Under grace, and not under law."*

We are told that, on this plane, a woman reaps where she has sown; the gifts of God are simply poured out upon her. "All that the Kingdom affords is hers." This continued state of bliss awaits the woman who has overcome the mortal thought.

In the mortal thought there is tribulation, but Jesus Christ said, "Be of good cheer; I have overcome the world."

Mortal thought is that of sin, sickness, and death. Jesus saw their absolute unreality and said sickness and sorrow shall pass away, and death itself, the last enemy, be overcome.

We know now, from a scientific standpoint, that death can be overcome by stamping the subconscious mind with the conviction of eternal youth and eternal life. The subconscious, being simply power without direction, *carries out orders without questioning.*

Working under the direction of the superconscious (the Christ or God within all), the "resurrection of the body" would be accomplished.

A woman will no longer throw off her body in death. Instead, it will be transformed into the "body electric," as sung by Walt Whitman, for Christianity is founded upon the forgiveness of sins and "an empty tomb."

**A woman cannot force the external to be
what she is not.**

A burden is an adverse thought or condition, and this thought or condition has its root in the subconscious.

❖

CHAPTER 6

Casting the Burden

Impressing the Subconscious

When a woman knows her own powers and the workings of her mind, her great desire is to find an easy and quick way to impress the subconscious with good, for simply an intellectual knowledge of the Truth will not bring results. In my own case, I found the easiest way is in *casting the burden*.

A metaphysician once explained it in this manner. He said, "The only thing that gives anything weight in nature is the law of gravitation, and if a boulder could be taken high above the planet, there would be no weight in that boulder; and that is what Jesus Christ meant when he said: 'My yoke is easy and my burden is light.'"

He had overcome the mortal thought, and functioned in the fourth dimensional realm, where there is only perfection, completion, life, and joy.

He said, "Come to me all ye that labor and are heavy laden, and I will give you rest . . . Take my yoke upon you, for my yoke is easy and my burden is light."

We are also told in the Fifty-Fifth Psalm, to "Cast thy burden upon the Lord." Many passages in the Bible state that the *battle is God's* and that a woman is always to *stand still and see the salvation of the Lord.*

This indicates that the superconscious mind (or Christ within) is the department that fights the battle and relieves the burdens. We see, therefore, that a woman violates Law if she carries a burden. A burden is an adverse thought or condition, and this thought or condition has its root in the subconscious.

It seems almost impossible to make any headway directing the subconscious from the conscious, or reasoning mind, as the reasoning mind (the intellect) is limited in its conceptions and filled with doubts and fears.

How scientific it then is to cast the burden upon the superconscious mind (or Christ within) where it is "made light," or dissolved into its "native nothingness."

For example: A woman in urgent need of money "made light" upon the Christ within, the superconscious, with the statement, "I cast this burden of lack on the Christ (within) and I go free to have plenty!" The belief in lack was her burden, and as she cast it upon the superconscious with its belief of plenty. An avalanche of supply was the result.

We read, "The Christ in you, the hope of glory."

Another example: One of my students had been given a new piano, and there was no room in her studio for it until she had moved out the old one. She was in a state of perplexity. She wanted to keep the old piano, but knew of no place to send it. She became desperate, since the new piano was to be sent immediately; in fact, it was on its way, with no place to put it. She said it came to her to repeat: "I cast this burden on the Christ within, and I go free."

A few moments later, her phone rang, and a friend asked if she might rent her old piano. It was moved out a few minutes before the new one arrived.

I knew a woman whose burden was resentment. She said: "I cast this burden of resentment on the Christ within, and I go free, to be loving, harmonious, and happy." The Almighty superconscious flooded the subconscious with love, and her whole life was changed. For years, resentment had held her in a state of torment and imprisoned her soul (the subconscious mind).

The statement should be made over and over and over, sometimes for hours at a time, silently or audibly, with quietness but determination. I have often compared it to winding-up an old clock. We must wind ourselves up with spoken words.

I have noticed, in "casting the burden," after a little while, one seems to see clearly. It is impossible to have clear vision while in the throes of carnal mind. doubts and fear poison the mind and body, and imagination runs riot, attracting disaster and disease.

In steadily repeating the affirmation — "I cast this burden on the Christ within, and go free," — the vision clears, and with it comes a feeling of relief, and sooner or later comes *the manifestation of good, be it health, happiness, or supply.*

One of my students once asked me to explain the "darkness before the dawn." I referred in a preceding chapter to the fact that often, before the big demonstration, "everything seems to go wrong," and deep depression clouds the consciousness. It means that out of the subconscious are rising the doubts and fears of the ages. These old derelicts of the subconscious rise to the surface, *to be put out.*

It is then that a woman should clap her cymbals, like Jehoshaphat, and give thanks that she is saved, even though she seems surrounded by the enemy (the situation of lack or disease). The student continued, "How long must one remain in the dark?" and I replied, "Until one can *see in the dark,*" for "*casting the burden enables one to see in the dark.*"

In order to impress the subconscious, active faith is always essential.

"Faith without works is dead." In these chapters I have endeavored to bring out this point. Jesus Christ showed active faith when "He commanded the multitude to sit down on the ground" before He gave thanks for the loaves and fishes.

I will give another example showing how necessary this step is. In fact, active faith is the bridge over which a woman passes to her Promised Land.

Through misunderstanding, a woman had been separated from her partner, who she loved deeply. Her partner refused all offers of reconciliation and would not communicate with her in any way.

Coming into the knowledge of Spiritual Law, she denied the appearance of separation. She made this statement: "There is no separation in Divine Mind, therefore, I cannot be separated from the love and companionship that are mine by Divine Right."

She showed active faith by keeping her in her thoughts every day, thereby impressing the subconscious with a picture of her return. Over a year passed, but she never wavered, and one day she walked in.

The subconscious is often impressed through music. Music has a fourth dimensional quality and releases the soul from imprisonment. It makes wonderful things seem *possible and easy of accomplishment!*

I have a friend who uses music daily, for this purpose. It puts her in perfect harmony and releases the imagination. Another woman often dances while making her affirmations. The rhythm and harmony of music and motion carry her words forth with tremendous power.

The student must remember also not to despise the "day of small things."

Invariably, before a demonstration, come "signs of land." Before Columbus reached America, he saw birds and twigs that showed him land was near. So it is with a demonstration; but often the student mistakes it for the demonstration itself and is disappointed.

For example: A woman had spoken the word for a set of

dishes. Not long afterward a friend gave her a dish that was old and cracked. She came to me and said, "Well, I asked for a set of dishes, and all I got was a cracked plate."

I replied, "The plate was only signs of land. It shows your dishes are coming — look upon it as a birds and seaweed." Not long afterward, the dishes came.

Continually "making believe" impresses the subconscious. If one makes believe she is rich, and makes believe she is successful, in "due time she will reap."

Children are always making believe, and "except ye be converted, and become as little children, ye shall not enter the Kingdom of Heaven."

For example: I know of a woman who was very poor, but no one could make her *feel* poor. She earned a small amount of money from rich friends who constantly reminded her of her poverty and to be careful and saving. Regardless of their admonitions, she would spend all her earnings on a hat, or make someone a gift, and be in a rapturous state of mind. Her thoughts were always centered on beautiful clothes and "rings and things," but without envying others.

She lived in the world of the wondrous, and only riches seemed real to her. Before long, she married a rich man, and the rings and things became visible. I do not know whether the man was her Divine Selection, but opulence had to manifest in her life, as she had imaged only opulence.

There is no peace or happiness for a woman until she has erased all fear from the subconscious. Fear is misdirected energy and must be redirected, or transmuted into Faith.

Jesus Christ said, "Why are ye fearful, O ye of little faith? . . . All things are possible to him that believeth."

I am asked so often by my students, "How can I get rid of fear?" I reply, "By walking up to the thing you are afraid of."

'The lion takes its fierceness from your fear." Walk up to the lion, and he will disappear; run away and he runs after you.

I have shown in previous chapters how the lion of lack disappeared when the individual spent money fearlessly, showing faith that God was her supply and, therefore, unfailing.

Many of my students have come out of the bondage of poverty and are now bountifully supplied through losing all fear of letting money go out. The subconscious is impressed with the truth that *God is the Giver and Gift*; therefore since one is one with the Giver, we are one with the Gift. A splendid statement is: "I now thank God the Giver for God the Gift."

When a woman has long separated herself from her good and her supply, through thoughts of separation and lack, sometimes it takes dynamite (a big situation) to dislodge these false ideas from her subconscious.

We see in the foregoing illustration how the individual was freed from her bondage by *showing fearlessness*.

Watch yourself hourly to detect if your motive for action is fear or faith.

Perhaps one's fear is of personality. Then do not avoid the people feared; be willing to meet them cheerfully, and they will either prove "golden links in the chain of one's good" or disappear harmoniously from one's pathway.

Perhaps one's fear is of disease or germs. Then one should be fearless and undisturbed in a germ-laden situation, and she would be immune.

One can only contract germs while vibrating at the same rate as the germ, and fear drags women down to the level of the germ. Of course, the disease- laden germ is the product of carnal mind, as all thought must objectify. Germs do not exist in the superconscious or Divine Mind, and therefore are the product of "vain imagination."

"In the twinkling of an eye," a woman's release will come when she realizes *there is no power in evil*.

The material world will fade away, and the fourth dimensional world, the "World of the Wondrous," will swing into manifestation.

"And I saw a new heaven, and a new Earth — and there shall be no more death, neither sorrow nor crying, neither shall there be any more pain; for the former things are passed away."

**Choose ye this day whom we shall serve,
fear or faith.**

Real love is selfless and free from fear.

Love

Every woman on this planet is taking her initiation in love. "A new commandment I give unto you, that ye love one another." Ouspensky states, in *Tertium Organum*, that "love is a cosmic phenomenon" and opens the fourth dimensional world, "The World of the Wondrous."

Real love is selfless and free from fear. Real love pours itself out upon the object of its affection without demanding any return. Its joy is in the joy of giving. Love is God in manifestation and the strongest magnetic force in the Universe.

Pure, unselfish love *draws to itself its own*; it does not need to seek or demand. Scarcely anyone has the faintest conception of real love. When people are selfish, tyrannical, or fearful in their affections, they lose the thing they love. Jealousy is the worst enemy of love, for the imagination runs riot, seeing the loved one attracted to another, and invariably these fears objectify if they are not neutralized.

For example: A woman came to me in deep distress. The one she loved – she called him "The Cap" because he was a captain — had left her for someone else and said he never intended to marry her. She was torn with jealousy and resentment and said she hoped he would suffer as he had made her suffer. She then added, "How could he leave me when I loved him so much?"

I replied, "You are not loving that man, you are hating him," and added, "*You can never receive what you have never given. Give a perfect love and you will receive a perfect love.* Perfect yourself on him. Give him a perfect, unselfish love, demanding nothing in return, do not criticize or condemn, and *bless him wherever he is.*"

She replied, "No, I won't bless him unless I know where he is!" she said. "Well," I said, "that is not real love."

"When you *send out real love,* real love will return to you, either from this man or an equivalent, for if this person is not the Divine Selection, you will not want him. As you are one with God, you are one with the love that belongs to you by Divine Right."

Several months passed and matters remained about the same, but she was working conscientiously with herself. I said, "When you are no longer disturbed by his cruelty, he will cease to be cruel, as you are attracting it through your own emotions."

Then I told her of a brotherhood in India who never said "Good morning" to each other. They used these words: "*I salute the Divinity in you.*" They saluted the divinity in everyone, and in the wild animals in the jungle, and they were never harmed, for they *saw only God in every* living thing. I said, "Salute the divinity in this man, and say: 'I see your Divine self only. I see you as God sees you, perfect, made the same in image and likeness.'"

She found she was becoming more poised and gradually losing her resentment. He was a Captain, and she always called him "The Cap."

One day, she said, suddenly, "*God bless the Cap wherever he may be.*"

I replied: "Now that is real love, and when you have

become a 'complete circle' and are no longer disturbed by the situation, you will have that love or attract its equivalent."

I was moving at this time and did not have a telephone, so was out of touch with her for a few weeks, when one morning I received a letter saying, "We are married."

At the earliest opportunity, I paid her a call. My first words were, "What happened?"

"Oh," she exclaimed, "a miracle! One day I woke up and all suffering had ceased. I saw him that evening and he asked me to marry him. We were married in about a week, and I have never seen a more devoted man."

There is an old saying: "*No one is your enemy, no one is your friend, everyone is your teacher.*"

So become impersonal and learn what each person has to teach, and soon you will learn your lessons and be free.

This woman's lover was teaching her selfless love, which everyone, sooner or later, must learn.

Suffering is not necessary for a woman's development; it is the result of violation of Spiritual Law, but few people seem able to rouse themselves from their "soul sleep" without it. When people are happy, they usually become selfish, and automatically the law of Karma is set in action. People often suffer loss through lack of appreciation.

I knew a woman who had a very nice husband, but she said often, "I don't care anything about being married, but that is nothing against my husband. I'm simply not interested in married life."

She had other interests and scarcely remembered she had a husband. She only thought of him when she saw him. One day her husband told her he was in love with another woman, and left. She came to me in distress and resentment.

I replied, "It is exactly what you spoke the word for. You said you didn't care anything about being married, so the subconscious worked to get you unmarried." She said, "Oh yes, I see. People get what they want, and then feel very much hurt."

She soon became in perfect harmony with the situation and knew they were both much happier apart.

A woman came to me dejected, miserable, and poor. Her close friend was interested in the "Science of Numbers" and had had her read. It seems the report was not very favorable, for she said, "My friend says I'll never amount to anything because I am a 'two.'"

I replied, "I don't care what your number is, you are a perfect idea in Divine Mind, and we will demand the success and prosperity that are *already planned* for you by Infinite Intelligence."

Within a few weeks, she had a very fine position, and a year or two later, she achieved a brilliant success as a writer.

No woman can attract money if she despises it. Many people are kept in poverty by saying, "Money means nothing to me, and I have a contempt for people who have it." This is the reason so many artists are poor. Their contempt for money separates them from it. I remember hearing one artist say of another, "She's no good as an artist; she has money in the bank."

This attitude of mind, of course, separates a woman from her supply; she must be in harmony with something in order to attract it.

Money is God in manifestation, as freedom from want and limitation, but it must be always kept in circulation and put to right uses. Hoarding and saving react with grim vengeance.

This does not mean that a woman should not have houses and lots, stocks and bonds, for "the life of the a righteous woman shall be full." It means a woman should not hoard even the principal if an occasion arises when money is necessary. In letting it go out fearlessly and cheerfully, she opens the way for more to come in, for God is the unfailing and inexhaustible supply.

This is the spiritual attitude toward money, and the great Bank of the Universal never fails!

We see an example of hoarding in the 1925 MGM film production of *Greed**. The woman won five thousand dollars in a lottery, but would not spend it. She hoarded and saved, let her husband suffer and starve, and eventually she scrubbed floors for a living. She loved the money itself and put it above everything, and one night she was murdered and the money taken from her.

This is an example of where "love of money is the root of all evil." Money in itself is good and beneficial, but used for destructive purposes, hoarded and saved, or considered more important than love, brings disease and disaster, and the loss of the money itself.

Follow the path of love, and all things are added, *for God is love and God is supply*; follow the path of selfishness and greed, and the supply vanishes or you become separated from it.

For example: I knew the case of a very rich woman who hoarded her income. She rarely gave anything away, but bought and bought things for herself.

---

* A more contemporary example might be found in the 1994 movie *It Could Happen to You*, where a police officer played by Nicholas Cage, does not have a tip for his coffee shop waitress, played by Bridget Fonda. Not wanting to leave without showing his appreciation, he offers to share his prize money if his lottery ticket is a winner. When he does win, his greedy wife takes him to court to sue for all of the winnings, and she is successful. But she is not the ultimate winner. Eventually she squanders everything, including her marriage. The police officer and the waitress find love and receive cash gifts from well-wishers that far exceed the amount they had originally won. In his efforts to share, the police officer is rewarded with abundance. The wife's greed and desire to take everything costs her everything.

She was very fond of necklaces, and a friend once asked her how many she possessed. She replied, "Sixty-seven." She bought them and put them away, carefully wrapped in tissue paper. Had she used the necklaces, it would have been quite legitimate, but she was violating the law of use. Her closets were filled with clothes she never wore and jewels that never saw the light.

The woman's arms were gradually becoming paralyzed from holding on to things. Eventually she was considered incapable of looking after her affairs, and her wealth was handed over to others to manage.

So people, in ignorance of the law, bring about their own destruction.

All disease, all unhappiness, come from the violation of the law of love. A woman's boomerangs of hate, resentment, and criticism come back laden with sickness and sorrow. Love seems almost a lost art, but the woman with the knowledge of Spiritual Law knows it must be regained, for without it, she has "become as sounding brass and tinkling cymbals."

For example: I had a student who came to me, month after month, to clean her consciousness of resentment. After a while, she arrived at the point where she resented only one woman, but that one woman kept her busy. Little by little she became poised and harmonious, and one day, all resentment was wiped out.

She came in radiant and exclaimed, "You can't understand how I feel! The woman said something to me and, instead of being furious, I was loving and kind, and she apologized and was perfectly lovely to me. No one can understand the marvelous lightness I feel within!"

Love and goodwill are invaluable in business.

For example: A woman came to me, complaining of her employer. She said she was cold and critical; the woman knew her empolyer did not want her in the position.

"Well," I replied, "salute the Divinity in the woman and send her love."

She said, "I can't; she's a marble woman."

I answered, "You remember the story of the sculptor who asked for a certain piece of marble? He was asked why he wanted it, and he replied, 'Because there is an angel in the marble,' and out of it he produced a wonderful work of art."

"Very well," she said, "I'll try it." A week later she came back and said, "I did what you told me to, and now the woman is very kind, she even took me out to lunch."

People are sometimes filled with remorse for having done someone an unkindness, perhaps years ago. If the wrong cannot be righted, its effect can be neutralized by doing some one a kindness *in the present*.

"This one thing I do, forgetting those things that are behind and reaching forth unto those things that are before."

Sorrow, regret, and remorse tear down the cells of the body and poison the atmosphere of the individual.

A woman said to me in deep sorrow, "Treat me to be happy and joyous, for my sorrow makes me so irritable with members of my family that I keep making more Karma."

I was asked to treat a woman who was mourning for her daughter. I denied all belief in loss and separation and affirmed that God was the woman's joy, love, and peace.

The woman gained her poise at once, but sent word by her son not to treat any longer because she was "so happy, it wasn't respectable."

Mortal mind loves to hang on to its griefs and regrets.

I knew a woman who went about bragging of her troubles, so, of course, she always had something to brag about.

The old idea was if a woman did not worry about her children, she was not a good mother. Now we know that mother-fear is responsible for many of the diseases and accidents that come into the lives of children. For fear pictures vividly the disease or situation feared, and these pictures objectify, if not neutralized.

Happy is the mother who can say sincerely that she puts her child in God's hands and *knows*, therefore, that she is divinely protected.

For example: A woman awoke suddenly in the night, feeling her brother was in great danger. Instead of giving in to her fears, she commenced making statements of Truth, saying: "We are a perfect idea in Divine Mind and are always in the right place. Therefore, my brother is in his right place and is divinely protected."

The next day she learned that her brother had been in close proximity to an explosion in a mine, but had miraculously escaped.

So a woman is her brother's keeper (in thought), and every woman should know that the thing she loves dwells in "the secret place of the most high and abides under the shadow of the Almighty."

"Perfect love casteth out fear. She that feareth is not made perfect in love."

Love is the fulfilling of the Law.
Follow the path of love.

Acknowledge God in all thy ways
and God shall direct thy path.

CHAPTER 8

Intuition or Guidance

There is nothing too great of accomplishment for the woman who knows the power of her word and who follows her intuitive leads. By the word, she starts in action unseen forces and can rebuild her body or remold her affairs. It is, therefore, of the utmost importance to choose the right words, and the student carefully selects the affirmation she wishes to catapult into the invisible. She knows that God is her supply, that there is a supply for every demand, and that her spoken word releases this supply.

"Ask and ye shall receive."

A woman must make the first move. "Draw nigh to God and God will draw nigh to you."

I have often been asked just how to make a demonstration.

I reply, "Speak the word and then do not do anything until you get a definite lead." Demand the lead, saying: "Infinite Spirit, reveal to me the way, let me know if there is anything for me to do."

The answer will come through intuition (or hunch), a chance remark from someone, or a passage in a book. The answers are sometimes quite startling in their exactness.

For example: A woman desired a large sum of money. She spoke the words: "Infinite Spirit, open the way for my immediate supply, let all that is mine by Divine Right now reach me, in great avalanches of abundance." Then she added: "Give me a definite lead, let me know if there is anything for me to do."

The thought came quickly: "Give a certain friend (who had helped her spiritually) a hundred dollars." She told her friend, who said, "Wait and get another lead, before giving it." So she waited, and that day met a woman who said to her, "I gave someone a dollar today; it was just as much for me, as it would be for you to give someone a hundred."

This was indeed an unmistakable lead, so she knew she was right in giving the hundred dollars. It was a gift that proved a great investment, for shortly after that, a large sum of money came to her in a remarkable way.

Giving opens the way for receiving. In order to create activity in finances, one should give. Tithing, or giving one-tenth of one's income, is an old Jewish custom and is sure to bring increase. Many of the richest people in this country have been tithers, and I have never known it to fail as an investment.

The tenth-part goes forth and returns blessed and multiplied. But the gift or tithe must be given with love and cheerfulness, for "God loveth a cheerful giver." Bills should be paid cheerfully, all money should be sent forth fearlessly and with a blessing.

This attitude of mind makes a woman master of money. It is hers to obey, and her spoken word then opens vast reservoirs of wealth.

A woman, herself, limits her supply by her limited vision. Sometimes the student has a great realization of wealth, but is afraid to act.

The vision and action must go hand in hand, as in the case of the woman who bought the expensive overcoat.

A woman came to me asking me to speak the word for a

position. So I demanded: "Infinite Spirit, open the way for this woman's right position." Never ask for just "a position"; ask for the *right* position, the place already planned in Divine Mind, as it is the only one that will give satisfaction.

I then gave thanks that she had already received and that it would manifest quickly. Very soon, she had three positions offered her, two in New York and one in Palm Beach, and she did not know which to choose. I said, "Ask for a definite lead."

The time was almost up and she was still undecided, when one day, she telephoned. "When I woke up this morning, I could smell Palm Beach," she said. She had been there before and knew its balmy fragrance.

I replied, "Well, if you can smell Palm Beach from here, it is certainly your lead." She accepted the position, and it proved a great success. Often one's lead comes at an unexpected time.

One day, I was walking down the street, when I suddenly felt a strong urge to go to a certain bakery, a block or two away.

The reasoning mind resisted, arguing, "There is nothing there that you want."

However, I had learned not to reason, so I went to the bakery, looked at everything, and there was certainly nothing there that I wanted. But coming out, I encountered a woman I had thought of often and who was in great need of the help that I could give her.

So often, one goes for one thing and finds another. Intuition is a spiritual faculty and does not explain, but simply *points the way*.

A person often receives a lead during a treatment. The idea that comes may seem quite irrelevant, but some of God's leadings are mysterious.

In the class one day, I was treating that each individual would receive a definite lead. A woman came to me afterward, and said, "While you were treating, I got the hunch to take my furniture out of storage and get an apartment." The woman had come to be treated for health. I told her I knew in getting a home of her own, her health would improve, and I added, "I believe your trouble, which is a congestion, has come from having things stored away. Congestion of things causes congestion in the body. You have violated the law of use, and your body is paying the penalty."

So I gave thanks that "Divine Order was established in her mind, body, and affairs."

People little dream of how their affairs react on the body. There is a mental correspondence for every disease. A person might receive instantaneous healing through the realization of her body being a perfect idea in Divine Mind, and, therefore, whole and perfect, but if she continues her destructive thinking, hoarding, hating, fearing, condemning, the disease will return.

Jesus Christ knew that all sickness came from sin, but admonished the leper, after the healing, to go and sin no more, lest a worse thing come.

The metaphysician is always delving deep for the correspondence in disease. In order to achieve total healing, the soul (or subconscious mind) must be washed whiter than snow.

Jesus Christ said, "Condemn not lest ye also be condemned . . . Judge not, lest ye be judged."

Many people have attracted disease and unhappiness through condemnation of others. What a woman condemns in others, she attracts to herself.

For example: A friend came to me in anger and distress because her husband had deserted her for another woman. She condemned the other woman and said continually, "She knew he was a married man and had no right to accept his attentions."

I replied, "Stop condemning the woman, bless her, and be through with the situation, otherwise, you are attracting the same thing to yourself." She was deaf to my words, and a year or two later, became deeply interested in a married man herself.

People pick up a live-wire whenever they criticize or condemn, and may expect a shock.

Indecision is a stumbling block in many a pathway. In order to overcome it, make the statement repeatedly: "I am always under direct inspiration; I make right decisions, quickly."

These words impress the subconscious, and soon one finds herself awake and alert, making her right moves without hesitation. I have found it destructive to look to the psychic plane for guidance, as it is the plane of many minds and not "The One Mind."

As a woman opens her mind to subjectivity, she becomes a target for destructive forces. The psychic plane is the result of our mortal thought and is on the "plane of opposites." She may receive either good or bad messages. The science of numbers and the reading of horoscopes, keep people down on the mental (or mortal) plane, for they deal only with the karmic path.

I know of a man who should have been dead, years ago, according to his horoscope, but he is alive and a leader of one of the biggest movements in this country for the uplift of humanity.

It takes a very strong mind to neutralize a prophecy of evil. The student should declare: "Every false prophecy shall come to naught; every plan God in heaven has not planned shall be dissolved and dissipated. The Divine Idea now comes to pass."

However, if any good message has ever been given one — of coming happiness or wealth — harbor and expect it, and it will manifest sooner or later through the law of expectancy.

A woman's will should be used to back the Universal will: "I will that the will of God be done."

It is God's will to give each woman every righteous desire of her heart, and her will should be used to hold the perfect vision, without wavering.

The prodigal son said: "I will arise and go to my Father."

It is, indeed, often an effort of the will to leave the husks and swine of mortal thinking. It is so much easier, for the average person, to have fear than faith; *so faith is an effort of the will.*

As a woman becomes spiritually awakened, she recognizes that any external inharmony is the correspondence of mental inharmony. If she stumbles or falls, she may know she is stumbling or falling in consciousness.

One day, a student was walking along the street condemning someone in her thoughts. She was saying mentally, "That woman is the most disagreeable woman on Earth," when suddenly three teenagers rushed around the corner and almost knocked her over. She did not condemn the teenagers, but immediately called on the law of forgiveness, and saluted the divinity in the woman. Wisdom's ways are ways of pleasantness and all her paths are peace.

When one has made her demands upon the Universal, she must be ready for surprises. Everything may seem to be going wrong, when in reality, it is going right.

For example: A woman was told that there was no loss in Divine Mind, therefore, she could not lose anything that belonged to her; anything lost, would be returned, or she would receive its equivalent.

Several years previously, she had lost two thousand dollars. She had loaned the money to a relative during her lifetime, but the relative had died, leaving no mention of it in her will. The woman was resentful and angry, and as she had no written statement of the transaction, she never received the money. So she determined to deny the loss and collect the two thousand dollars from the Bank of the Universal. She had to begin by forgiving the woman, as resentment and unforgiveness close the doors of this wonderful bank.

She made this statement: "I deny loss, there is no loss in Divine Mind, therefore, I cannot lose the two thousand dollars, which belong to me by Divine Right. *As one door shuts another door opens.*"

She was living in an apartment house that was for sale. In the lease was a clause stating that if the house was sold, the tenants would be required to move out within ninety days.

Suddenly, the landlord broke the lease and raised the rent. Again, injustice was on her pathway, but this time she was undisturbed. She blessed the landlord, and said: "Since the rent has been raised, it means that I'll be that much richer, for God is my supply."

New leases were made out for the advanced rent, but by some divine mistake, the ninety days clause had been forgotten. Soon after, the landlord had an opportunity to sell the house. On account of the mistake in the new leases, the tenants held possession for another year.

The agent offered each tenant two hundred dollars to vacate. Several families moved; three remained, including the woman. A month or two passed, and the agent again appeared. This time he said to the woman, "Will you break your lease for the sum of fifteen hundred dollars?" It flashed upon her, "Here comes the two thousand dollars." She remembered having said to friends in the house, "We will all act together if anything more is said about leaving." So her *lead* was to consult her friends.

These friends said," Well, if they have offered you fifteen hundred they will certainly give two thousand." So she received a check for two thousand dollars for giving up the apartment. It was certainly a remarkable working of the Law, and the apparent injustice was merely opening the way for her demonstration.

It proved that there is no loss, and when a woman takes her spiritual stand, she collects all that is hers from this great Reservoir of Good.

"I will restore to you the years the locusts have eaten." The locusts are the doubts, fears, resentments, and regrets of mortal thinking.

These adverse thoughts, alone, are self-defeating, for "No woman gives to herself but herself, and no woman takes away from herself but herself."

People are here to prove God and "to bear witness to the Truth," and they can only prove God by bringing plenty out of lack and justice out of injustice.

"Prove me now herewith, saith the Lord of hosts, if I will not open you the windows of heaven, and pour out a blessing, that there shall not be room enough to receive it."

The vision and action must go hand in hand.

There is, for each woman,
perfect self-expression.

CHAPTER 9

Perfect Self-Expression or The Divine Design

There is a place that each woman is to fill and no one else can fill; something that she is to do, that no one else can do. It is her destiny!

This achievement is held a perfect idea in Divine Mind, awaiting each woman's recognition. As the imaging faculty is the creative faculty, it is necessary for a woman to see the idea before it can manifest. So a woman's highest demand is for the *Divine Design of her life*.

She may not have the faintest conception of what it is, for there is, possibly, some marvelous talent hidden deep within her.

Her demand should be: "Infinite Spirit, open the way for the Divine Design of my life to manifest; let the genius within me now be released; let me see clearly the perfect plan."

The perfect plan includes health, wealth, love, and perfect self-expression. This is the *square of life*, which brings perfect happiness. When one has made this demand, she may find great changes taking place in her life, for nearly every woman has wandered far from the Divine Design.

In one woman's case, it was as though a cyclone had struck her affairs. But readjustments came quickly, and new and wonderful conditions took the place of old ones.

Perfect self-expression will never be labor, but of such absorbing interest that it will seem almost like play. The student knows, also, since a woman comes into the world financed by God, the *supply* needed for her perfect self-expression will be at hand.

Many a genius has struggled for years with the problem of supply, when her spoken word, and faith, would have quickly released the necessary funds.

For example: After class one day, a woman came to me and handed me a cent. She said, "I have just seven cents in the world, and I'm going to give you one; for I have faith in the power of your spoken word. I want you to speak the word for my perfect self-expression and prosperity."

I spoke the word and did not see her again until a year later. She came in one day, successful and happy, with a roll of money in her pocket. She said, "Immediately after you spoke the word, I had a position offered me in a distant city, and am now demonstrating health, happiness, and supply."

A woman's perfect self-expression may be in becoming a perfect mother, a perfect homemaker, or a perfect career-woman.

Demand definite leads and the way will be made easy and successful.

One should not visualize or force a mental picture. When a woman demands the Divine Design to come into her conscious mind, she will receive flashes of inspiration and begin to see herself making some great accomplishment. This is the picture, or idea, she must hold without wavering.

The thing a woman seeks is seeking her — *the telephone was seeking Bell!*

Parents should never force careers and professions upon their children. With a knowledge of Spiritual Truth, the Divine Plan could be spoken for early in childhood or prenatally.

A prenatal treatment should be: "Let the God in this child have perfect expression; let the Divine Design of mind, body, and affairs be made manifest throughout life, throughout eternity."

God's will be done, not ours; God's pattern, not our pattern is the command we find running through all the scriptures, and the Bible is a book dealing with the science of the mind. It is a book telling people how to release their soul (or subconscious mind) from bondage.

The battles described are pictures of people waging war against mortal thoughts. "Foes shall be they of their own household." Everyone is Jehoshaphat, and everyone is David who slays Goliath (mortal thinking) with the little white stone (faith).

So a woman must be careful that she is not the "wicked and slothful servant" who buried her talent. There is a terrible penalty to be paid for not using one's ability.

Often fear stands between a woman and her perfect self-expression. Stage-fright has hampered many a genius. This may be overcome by the spoken word or treatment. The individual then loses all self-consciousness and feels simply that she is a channel for Infinite Intelligence to express Itself through.

She is under direct inspiration, fearless, and confident; for she feels that it is the "God within" her who does the work.

A young girl came often to my class with her mother. She asked me to speak the word for her coming examinations at school.

I told her to make the statement: "I am one with Infinite Intelligence. I know everything I should know on this subject." She had an excellent knowledge of history, but was not sure of her arithmetic. I saw her afterward, and she said, "I spoke the word for my arithmetic and passed with the highest honors; but I thought I could depend on myself for history, and instead got a very poor mark." A woman often receives a setback when she is too sure of herself, which means she is trusting her personality and not the God within.

Another one of my students gave me an example of this. She took an extended trip abroad one summer, visiting many countries where she was ignorant of the languages. She was calling for guidance and protection every minute, and her affairs went smoothly and miraculously. Her luggage was never delayed nor lost! Accommodations were always ready for her at the best hotels; and she had perfect service wherever she went. She returned to New York. Knowing the language, she felt God was no longer necessary, so looked after her affairs in an ordinary manner.

Everything went wrong, her trunks delayed, amid inharmony and confusion. The student must form the habit of practicing the presence of God every minute. "In all thy ways acknowledge God," for nothing is too small or too great.

Sometimes an insignificant incident may be the turning point in a woman's life.

Robert Fulton, watching some boiling water simmering in a tea kettle, saw a steamboat!

I have seen a student often keep back her demonstration through resistance. She pins her faith to one channel only and dictates just the way she desires the manifestation to come, which brings things to a standstill.

"My way, not your way!" is the command of Infinite Intelligence. Like all power, be it steam or electricity, it must have a nonresistant engine or instrument to work through, and people are the engines or instruments.

Over and over again, one is told to stand still. "Oh, Judah, fear not; but tomorrow go out against them, for the Lord will be with you. You shall not need to fight this battle; set yourselves, stand ye still, and see the salvation of the Lord with you."

We see this in the incidents of the two thousand dollars coming to the woman through the landlord when she became *nonresistant* and *undisturbed*, and the woman who won the man's love after "all suffering had ceased."

The student's goal is *poise!*

Poise is power, for it gives God-Power a chance to rush through, to "will and to do Its good pleasure." Poised, she thinks clearly, and makes "right decisions quickly . . . She never misses a trick."

Anger blurs the vision, poisons the blood, is the root of many diseases, and causes wrong decision leading to failure.

It has been named one of the worst "sins," since its reaction is so harmful. The student learns that, in metaphysics, sin has a much broader meaning than in the old teaching. "Whatsoever is not of faith is sin."

One finds that fear and worry are deadly sins. They are inverted faith, and through distorted mental pictures, bring to pass the thing most feared. The work is to drive out these enemies (from the subconscious mind). "When we are *fearless we are finished!*" Maurice Maeterlinck (who was awarded the Nobel Prize for Literature in 1911) says that "Man is God afraid."

So, as we read in the previous chapters, a woman can only vanquish fear by walking up to the thing she is afraid of. When Jehoshaphat and his army prepared to meet the enemy, singing "Praise the Lord, for mercy endureth forever," they found their enemies had destroyed each other, and there was nothing to fight.

For example: A woman asked a friend to deliver a message to another friend. The woman feared to give the message, since the reasoning mind said, "Don't get mixed up in this affair, don't give that message."

She was troubled in spirit, for she had given her promise. At last, she determined to "walk up to the lion" and call on the law of divine protection. She met the friend to whom she was to deliver the message. She opened her mouth to speak it, when her friend said, "So-and-So has left town." This made it unnecessary to give the message, since the situation depended upon the person being in town. As she was willing to do it, she was not obliged to; as she did not fear, the situation vanished.

The student often delays her demonstration through a belief in incompletion. She should make this statement: "In Divine Mind there is only completion, therefore, my demonstration is completed. My perfect work, my perfect home, my perfect health." Whatever she demands are perfect ideas registered in Divine Mind and must manifest "under grace in a perfect way." She gives thanks she has already received on the invisible, and makes active preparation for receiving on the visible.

One of my students was in need of a financial demonstration. She came to me and asked why it was not completed.

I replied, "Perhaps you are in the habit of leaving things unfinished, and the subconscious has gotten into the habit of not completing (as the without, so the within)."

She said, "You are right. I often begin things and never finish them. I'll go home and finish something I commenced weeks ago, and I know it will be symbolic of my demonstration."

She sewed assiduously, and the article was soon completed. Shortly after, the money came in a most curious manner. Her husband was paid his salary twice that month. He told his employers of their mistake, and they sent word to keep it.

When a woman asks, *believing, she must receive, for God creates God's own channels!*

I have been sometimes asked, "Suppose one has several talents. How is she to know which one to choose?" Demand to be shown definitely. Say: "Infinite Spirit, give me a definite lead, reveal to me my perfect self-expression, show me which talent I am to make use of now."

I have known people to suddenly enter a new line of work

and be fully equipped, with little or no training. So make the statement: "I am fully equipped for the Divine Plan of my life," and be fearless in grasping opportunities.

Some people are cheerful givers, but bad receivers. They refuse gifts through pride or some negative reason, thereby blocking their channels, and invariably find themselves eventually with little or nothing.

For example: A woman who had given away a great deal of money had a gift offered her of several thousand dollars. She refused to take it, saying she did not need it. Shortly after that, her finances were "tied up," and she found herself in debt for that amount. A woman should receive gracefully the bread returning to her upon the water — freely ye have given, freely ye shall receive.

There is always the perfect balance of giving and receiving, and though a woman should give without thinking of returns, she violates Law if she does not accept the returns that come to her; for all gifts are from God, people being merely the channel.

A thought of lack should never be held over the giver.

For example: When the woman gave the one cent, I did not say, "Poor woman, she cannot afford to give me that." I saw her rich and prosperous, with her supply pouring in. It was this thought that brought it. If one has been a bad receiver, she must become a good one, and take even a postage stamp if it is given her, and open up her channels for receiving.

The Lord loveth a cheerful receiver, as well as a cheerful giver.

I have often been asked why one is born rich and healthy, and another poor and sick. Where there is an effect there is always a cause; there is no such thing as chance.

This question is answered through the law of reincarnation. A woman goes through many births and deaths, until she knows the truth that sets her free. She is drawn back to the Earth plane through unsatisfied desire, to pay her karmic debts, or to "fulfill her destiny."

The woman born rich and healthy has had pictures in her subconscious mind, in her past life, of health and riches; and the poor and sick woman, of disease and poverty. A woman manifests, on any plane, the sum total of her subconscious beliefs.

However, birth and death are mortal laws, for the "wages of sin is death." The real woman, spiritual woman, is birthless and deathless! She never was born and has never died — "As she was in the beginning, she is now, and ever shall be!"

So through the Truth, a woman is set free from the law of Karma, sin, and death, bringing into manifestation the Divine Design of her life.

The Lord will say unto her, "Well done, thou good and faithful servant. Thou has been faithful over a few things, I will make thee ruler over many things (death itself); enter thou into the joy of thy Lord (eternal life)."

A woman's freedom comes through fulfilling her destiny.

Be ye transformed by the renewing of your mind.

CHAPTER 10

Denials and Affirmations

All the good that is to be made manifest in a woman's life is already an accomplished fact in Divine Mind and is released through a woman's recognition or spoken word. So she must be careful to decree that only the Divine Idea be made manifest, for often, she decrees, through her "idle words," failure or misfortune.

It is, therefore, of the utmost importance to word one's demands correctly, as stated in a previous chapter. If one desires a home, friend, position, or any other good thing, make the demand for the Divine Selection.

For example: "Infinite Spirit, open the way for my right home, my right friend, my right position. I give thanks *it now manifests under grace in a perfect way.*"

The latter part of the statement is most important.

For example: I knew a woman who demanded a thousand dollars. Her daughter was injured and they received a thousand dollars indemnity, so it did not come in a "perfect way." The demand should have been worded in this way: "Infinite Spirit, I give thanks that the one thousand dollars, which is mine by Divine Right, is now released, and reaches me under grace in a perfect way."

As one grows in a financial consciousness, she should demand that the enormous sums of money, which are hers by Divine Right, reach her under grace, in perfect ways.

It is impossible for a woman to release more than she thinks is possible, for one is bound by the limited expectancies of the subconscious. She must enlarge her expectancies in order to receive in a larger way.

A woman so often limits herself in her demands.

For example: A student made the demand for six hundred dollars, by a certain date. She did receive it, but heard afterward, that she came very near receiving a thousand dollars. She was given just six hundred, as the result of her spoken word.

"They limited the Holy One of Israel." Wealth is a matter of consciousness. The French have a legend giving an example of this. A poor man was walking along a road when he met a traveler, who stopped him and said, "My good friend, I see you are poor. Take this gold nugget, sell it, and you will be rich all your days."

The man was overjoyed at his good fortune and took the nugget home. He immediately found work and became so prosperous that he did not sell the nugget. Years passed, and he became a very rich man. One day he met a poor man on the road. He stopped him and said, "My good friend, I will give you this gold nugget, which, if you sell, will make you rich for life." The beggar took the nugget, had it valued, and found it was only brass. So we see, the first man became rich through feeling rich, thinking the nugget was gold.

Every woman has within herself a gold nugget; *it is her consciousness of gold, of opulence, that brings riches into her life.* In making her demands, a woman begins at her *journey's end*, simply by declaring she *has already received.* "Before ye call I shall answer."

Continually affirming establishes the belief in the subconscious. Here are some suggested affirmations that provide specific direction.

PROSPERITY

God is my unfailing supply, and large sums of money come to me quickly, under grace, in perfect ways.

❖

DIVINE IDEA

Every plan not planned by God shall be dissolved and dissipated, and the Divine Idea now comes to pass.

❖

TRUTH

Only that which is true of God is true of me,
for I and God are ONE.

❖

FAITH

As I am one with God, I am one with my good, for God is both the Giver and the Gift. I cannot separate the Giver from the Gift.

❖

DIVINE LOVE

Divine Love now dissolves and dissipates every wrong condition in my mind, body, and affairs. Divine Love is the most powerful chemical in the Universe and dissolves everything that is not of itself!

❖

HEALTH

Divine Love floods my consciousness with health, and every cell
in my body is filled with Light.

❖

CLEAR EYESIGHT

My eyes are God's eyes, I see with the eyes of Spirit. I see
clearly the open way. There are no obstacles on my pathway. I
see clearly the perfect plan.

❖

GUIDANCE

I am divinely sensitive to my intuitive leads and give instant
obedience to Thy will.

❖

THE HEARING IMPAIRED

My ears are God's ears, I hear with the ears of Spirit. I am nonresistant and am willing to be led. I hear glad tidings of great joy.

❖

THE RIGHT CAREER

I have perfect work
In a perfect way;
I give perfect service
For perfect pay.

❖

FREEDOM FROM ALL RESTRAINT

I cast this burden on the Christ within, and I go free!

❖

It would not be necessary to make an affirmation more than once if one had perfect faith! One should not plead or supplicate, but give thanks repeatedly, that she has received.

"The desert shall *rejoice* and blossom as the rose." This rejoicing that is yet in the desert (state of consciousness) opens the way for release. The Lord's Prayer is in the form of command and demand — "Give us this day our daily bread, and forgive us our debts as we forgive our debtors," — and ends in praise — "For thine is the Kingdom and the Power and the Glory, forever. Amen."

"Concerning the works of my hands, command ye me." So prayer is command and demand, praise and thanksgiving. The student's work is in making herself believe that "with God, all things are possible."

This is easy enough to state in the abstract, but a little more difficult when confronted with a problem.

For example: It was necessary for a woman to demonstrate a large sum of money within a stated time. She knew she must *do something* to get a realization (for realization is a manifestation), and she demanded a "lead."

She was walking through a department store when she saw a very beautiful pink enamel letter opener. She felt the "pull" toward it. The thought came, "I haven't a letter opener good enough to open letters containing large checks."

So she bought the letter opener, which the reasoning mind would have called an extravagance. When she held it in her hand, she had a flash of a picture of herself opening an envelope containing a large checks and, in a few weeks, she received the money. The pink letter opener was her bridge of active faith.

Many stories are told of the power of the subconscious when directed in faith.

For example: A man was spending the night in a farmhouse. The windows of the room had been nailed down, and in the middle of the night he felt suffocated and made his way in the dark to the window. He could not open it, so he smashed the pane with his fist, drew in draughts of fine fresh air, and had a wonderful night's sleep.

The next morning, he found he had smashed the glass of a bookcase and the window had remained closed during the whole night. He had *supplied himself with oxygen, simply by his thought of oxygen.*

When a student starts out to demonstrate, she should never turn back. "Let not that a woman who wavers think that she shall receive anything of the Lord."

A student once made this wonderful statement: "When I ask God for anything, I put my foot down, and I say, 'God, I'll take nothing less than I've asked for, but more!'" So a woman should never compromise. "Having done all — Stand." This is sometimes the most difficult time of demonstrating. The temptation comes to give up, to turn back, to compromise.

"God also serves who only stands and waits."

Demonstrations often come at the eleventh hour because that's when people tend to let go, that is, stop reasoning, and Infinite Intelligence has a chance to work.

Dreary desires are answered drearily, and impatient desires, long delayed or violently fulfilled.

For example: A woman asked me why it was she was constantly losing or breaking her glasses.

We found she often said to herself and others with vexation, "I wish I could get rid of my glasses." So her impatient desire was violently fulfilled. What she should have demanded was perfect eyesight, but what she registered in the subconscious was simply the impatient desire to be rid of her glasses; so they were continually being broken or lost.

Two attitudes of mind cause loss: depreciation, as in the case of the woman who did not appreciate her spouse, *or fear of loss*, which makes a picture of loss in the subconscious.

When a student is able to let go of her problem (cast her burden), she will have an instantaneous manifestation.

For example: A woman was out during a very stormy day and her umbrella was blown inside-out. She was about to make a call on some people whom she had never, met and she did not wish to make her first appearance with a dilapidated umbrella. She could not throw it away, since it did not belong to her. So in desperation, she exclaimed, "Oh, God, you take charge of this umbrella. I don't know what to do."

A moment later, a voice behind her said, "Lady, do you want your umbrella mended?" There stood an umbrella mender. She replied, "Indeed, I do."

The gentleman mended the umbrella while she went into the house to pay her call, and when she returned, she had a good umbrella. So there is always an umbrella mender at hand on a woman's pathway, when one puts the umbrealla (or situation) in God's hands.

One should always follow a denial with an affirmation.

For example: I was called on the phone late one night to treat a woman who I had never seen. She was apparently very ill. I made the statement: "I deny this appearance of disease. It is unreal, therefore cannot register in her consciousness; this woman is a perfect idea in Divine Mind, pure substance expressing perfection."

There is no time or space, in Divine Mind, therefore the word reaches instantly its destination and does not "return void." I have treated patients in Europe and have found that the result was instantaneous.

I am asked so often the difference between visualizing and visioning. Visualizing is a mental process governed by the reasoning or conscious mind; visioning is a spiritual process, governed by intuition, or the superconscious mind. The student should train her mind to receive these flashes of inspiration, and work out the divine pictures, through definite leads. When a woman can say: "I desire only that which God desires for me," her new set of blueprints is given her by the Master Architect, the God within. God's plan for each person transcends the limitation of the reasoning mind, and is always the square of life, containing health, wealth, love, and perfect self-expression. Many a woman is building for herself in imagination a bungalow when she should be building a palace.

If a student tries to force a demonstration (through the reasoning mind), she brings it to a standstill. "I will hasten it," saith the Lord. She should act only through intuition or definite leads. "Rest in the Lord and wait patiently. Trust also in the Lord, and the Lord will bring it to pass."

I have seen the Law work in the most astonishing manner.

For example: A student stated that it was necessary for her to have a hundred dollars for the following day. It was a debt of vital importance that had to be met. I spoke the word, declaring Spirit was never too late and that the supply was at hand.

That evening she phoned me of the miracle. She said that the thought came to her to go to her safe-deposit box at the bank to examine some papers. She looked over the papers, and at the bottom of the box was a new one hundred dollar bill. She was astounded and said she knew she had never put it there, for she had gone through the papers many times. It may have been a materialization, as Jesus Christ materialized the loaves and fishes. A woman will reach the stage where her "word is made flesh," or materialized, instantly. "The fields, ripe with the harvest," will a manifest immediately, as in all of the miracles of Jesus Christ.

There is a tremendous power alone in the name Jesus Christ. It stands for *Truth Made Manifest*. He said, "Whatsoever ye ask the Lord, in my name, the Lord will give it to you."

The power of this name raises the student into the fourth dimension, where she is freed from all astral and psychic influences, and she becomes "unconditioned and absolute, in the same way that God is unconditioned and absolute."

I have seen many healings accomplished by using the words, "In the name of Jesus Christ." He was both person and principle; and the Christ within each woman is her Redeemer and Salvation.

The Christ within is our own fourth dimensional self, the inner-self made in God's image and likeness. This is the self that has never failed, never known sickness or sorrow, was never born and has never died. It is the "resurrection and the life" of everyone! This means that God, the Universal, becomes the Christ in us. So daily, we are manifesting Christ within.

A woman should make an art of thinking. The Master Thinker is an artist and is careful to paint only the Divine Designs upon the canvas of her mind; and she paints these pictures with masterly strokes of power and decision, having perfect faith that there is no power to mar their perfection and that they shall manifest in her life the ideal made real. The simple rules are fearless faith, nonresistance and love!

May each reader be now freed from that thing that has held her in bondage through the ages, standing between her and her own, and "know the Truth that makes her free" — free to fulfill her destiny, to bring into a manifestation the *Divine Design of her life,* Health, Wealth, Love and Perfect Self-Expression.

**All power is given to each woman
to bring "her heaven" upon "her Earth" through right
thinking. This is the goal of the Game of Life.**

THANK YOU!

for selecting this book from DeVorss Publications. If you would like to receive a complete catalog of our specialized selection of current and classic Metaphysical, Spiritual, Inspirational, Self-Help, and New Thought books, please visit our website or give us a call and ask for your free copy.

DeVorss Publications
devorss.com • 800-843-5743